ICHIRO'S

Art of

PLAYING BASEBALL

Never allow adversity to have an effect on your mood and disposition from one at-bat to the next.

ICHIRO'S
Art of
PLAYING BASEBALL

◄ Learn How to Hit, Steal, and Field Like an All-Star ►

Jim Rosenthal

Photography by Tom DiPace

St. Martin's Griffin

New York

www.stmartins.com

BOOK DESIGN BY AMANDA DEWEY

ISBN 0-312-35831-8
EAN 978-0-312-35831-0

First Edition: May 2006

1 3 5 7 9 10 8 6 4 2

ACKNOWLEDGMENTS

Special thanks to Alex Rodriguez; Michael Homler—a very astute editor—and George Witte at St. Martin's Press; the Alpert family of Tokyo for their help in translation; Middlebury College for its excellent Japanese Department and superb library and research facility; Lou Piniella; Mike Cameron; John Olerud; Sam Perlozzo; Keith Hernandez; Tony Gwynn; Narumi Komatsu; and Ichiro Suzuki for his inspiration and knowledge of baseball.

FOREWORD

Ichiro is more than just a great hitter—he is the perfect example of an artist who knows how to make adjustments at the plate to help his team win games. I honestly believe that he could hit more home runs if he wanted to go that route, but at the end of the day the name of the game is winning, and Ichiro—a hitting machine—will not sacrifice his ability to put the bat on the ball, spray hits to all fields, and do whatever it takes to reach base.

One of the lessons any hitter can learn from Ichiro is his work ethic; he is always studying the pitcher to uncover weak spots. The amazing thing about him is that he was willing to change his hitting style when he left Japan to play for the Seattle Mariners in 2001. He knew that what worked in Japan was not working in spring training in 2001, and that's when he went back to a hitting style from an earlier stage of his career—before he made it to the pros in Japan.

Ichiro has said that when he played for the Orix Blue Wave, he would lift his right foot to coincide with the natural pause in the pitcher's delivery. But in the U.S.A. our major-league pitchers don't pause as much before releasing the pitch, and this messed up Ichiro's sense of timing. He made a simple and inspired adjustment in his timing by eliminating one part of his hitting sequence—he no longer lifted his right leg before initiating his swing.

Trust me, this type of change is not as easy as it seems. When you play baseball for many years, you start to rely on a mix of instinct and the sum total of your experience in deciding what to do and what not to do at the plate. A hitter is endlessly searching for a comfort zone, a sense of confidence that he can see the pitch coming out of the pitcher's hand—and the elusive dream is that the ball looks as big as a Florida grapefruit!

I had the pleasure of meeting Ichiro for the first time in 1999 when he spent two weeks working out in the Seattle Mariners' spring training camp. Though we communicated mostly through an interpreter, I was so impressed with his intelligence and his grasp of the fundamentals of the game.

Watching Ichiro play is a pleasure, although it would be much easier to have him on my team than trying to deal with watching our pitching staff attempt (often in vain) to get him out. Ichiro can reach pitches in the dirt and invent hits out of sinkers that would strike out almost anyone else in baseball.

Why? He is so fast and so secure in his fundamentals. He has a batting style that is unique, original, and yet an excellent model to learn from to master the art of hitting. No one else in the game today is a better pure hitter. And no one is a better role model for the next generation of All-Star talent—in the United States, Japan, Latin America . . . and wherever baseball is played, enjoyed, and appreciated for its beauty and simplicity.

—*Alex Rodriguez*
Coral Gables, Florida

PREFACE

Ichiro is more than just a superstar in Japan and the United States. In 2001, he became the first Japanese position player to make it on the scene in the major leagues. Not surprisingly, Ichiro duplicated, and in some cases surpassed, his impressive stats in Japan. He shocked American baseball fans with his superb grasp of the fundamentals of the game: He could make contact with pitches in the dirt; he could run to first base faster than any player in baseball, from home to first base in 3.6 seconds; and he had the most accurate arm, with circus catches an almost-daily part of his repertoire. To understand where Ichiro came from, there is a time line on page 1 of highlights and significant developments in Japanese professional baseball since the end of World War II.

ICHIRO'S

Art of

PLAYING BASEBALL

JAPANESE BASEBALL TIME LINE

November 23, 1945:

The first postwar baseball game was played at Jingu Stadium in Tokyo in front of 5,878 fans. The attraction on this chilly afternoon was an East vs. West grudge match.

1946–1948:

In 1946, eight teams participated in a full season of 105 games. Over the next few years, new teams, name changes, and mergers energized an evolving sport. And in 1948, a new baseball federation was established.

1949:

Several new teams petitioned to join the new federation, and the leaders of the existing teams split over whether or not to okay the expansion. This "disagreement" led to the formation of two distinct leagues: the Pacific Coast League (teams favorable to expansion) and the Central League (teams against the expansion). The Central League included the Yomiuri Giants and the Hanshin Tigers, two of the cornerstone franchises of Japanese professional baseball.

1951:

A former public prosecutor was named the first baseball commissioner.

And in Okayama, Japan, on November 13, 1951, a team of Pacific League All-Stars defeated a team of American League players. This was the first time that a Japanese team defeated an American team in a major-league baseball contest, and the victory created a sensation—and resurgent interest in pro baseball—in Japan.

1959:

Tadashi Sugiura of the Nankai Hawks pitched in 42 games, winning 38. He then pitched four more games—winning all four—against the Yomiuri Giants in the Japan Series. He was washed up by the age of twenty-six, his arm having been ruined by extreme overwork by his manager. This case study ultimately led to a modification of the way pitching staffs were handled in Japan in the 1970s.

Yutaka Enatsu, another great Japanese pitcher of the era, once was so overworked during a Japanese League season that he decided to protest what he called "the boot-camp conditions" by lying down on the practice field and sleeping while his teammates were put through their paces. Enatsu managed to get his manager fired through these antics, and was eventually converted to relief pitching. He finished his career with 193 saves, 206 wins, and 2,987 strikeouts.

1962:

Japanese legendary slugger Sadaharu Oh began his collaboration with Mr. Hiroshi Arakawa, the noted Zen hitting instructor who taught Oh the art of "downswinging" on the baseball that was to transform him into the Babe Ruth of Japan.

Oh on the technical points of downswinging:

"The bat head should swing over the shortest course possible to meet the ball. A pitch travels across a distance of more than sixty feet at speeds approaching 90 miles an hour [this speed was considered the zenith of power pitching in the early sixties]. The time involved is less than a half second, which means the ball will be by you before you can say yes or no. Therefore, the tip of the bat, which starts out above the strike zone, must travel the shortest course if you are to have any hope of hitting the baseball. That is what is known as downswinging.

"My big weakness was that I had a 'hitch' in my swing. This hitch grew more, not less, pronounced with time, so that in the beginning of my fourth year as a pro, it was very deeply ingrained. Arakawa-san's theory of downswinging was well suited to meet this problem. All that was really required was to cut out the 'extras' in my swing. If I learned to bring the bat head across the plate in the most direct line, my hitch would be gone."

1970:

The San Francisco Giants made a rare spring training trip to Japan, where the men in black and orange took a beating at the hands of the Nippon Professional Baseball (NPB) All-Star team. After the NPB All-Stars won six of nine over the Giants, manager Tetsuhara Kawakami of the NPB boasted, "The Americans have nothing more to teach us."

1971:

The Baltimore Orioles toured Japan after losing to the Pittsburgh Pirates in Game 7 of the World Series. Despite Kawakami's bold statement the previous spring, the O's won twelve of fourteen games over Japanese teams, including an eight-for-eight sweep of the Yomiuri Giants. Pat Dobson pitched three shutouts, including a no-hitter against the Giants, and the O's hurlers held Sadaharu Oh to a .111 batting average.

1987:

Sachio Kinugasa smashed Lou Gehrig's all-time consecutive-game streak, a mark that many thought would never be broken. Kinugasa's streak came to an end at 2,215, and was later eclipsed by Cal Ripken Jr. on June 14, 1996. (Kinugasa was in attendance.)

1990:

Japan once again beat a squad of major-league All-Stars four games to three, the second time Japan had won a tour victory over the United States (1970, of course, being the other).

1997:

Nigel Wilson, best known for being the Florida Marlins' first pick in the expansion draft, became only the fourth player to hit four home runs in a Japanese League game. Wilson, a lefty swinger who smashed four homers for the Nippon Ham Fighters, joined Yoshiyuki Iwamoto of the Shochiku Robins (1951), Sadaharu Oh of the Yomiuri Giants (1964), and Tony Solaita of the Nippon Ham Fighters (1980) in the elite four-homer club.

1998:

Kazuhiro Sasaki, the career and single-season record holder for saves in pro ball in Japan, set the new mark of 45 saves along with a sparkling 0.64 ERA while leading the Yokohama Bay Stars of the Central League to the Japan Series championship.

2000:

Sasaki paved the way for Ichiro with a brilliant debut with the Seattle Mariners. Sasaki who saved 229 games in over a decade with the Yokohama Bay Stars, broke into the major leagues with 37 saves for Seattle. This total eclipsed Todd Worrell's rookie record of 36 saves.

1994–2000:

Ichiro compiled the following batting averages in his last seven years playing in Japan: .385, .342, .356, .345, .358, .343, and .387. His seven consecutive batting titles outpaced the four straight won by Isao Harimoto from 1967 to 1970.

INTRO TO ICHIRO

*A Guide to Choosing the Right Equipment
and Other Insights**

Favorite Spikes:

The goal is to wear something that feels so light it is almost like running bare-
foot. I asked the designers at Asics (a sporting goods company in Japan) to find
the lightest compounds, and they came up with a model that weighs only 5.3
ounces per shoe. The last year I played in Japan I was using spikes that had leather
soles with metal spikes. In America the playing fields are harder, so I switched to
the model made with a plastic resin instead of leather. The leather sops may be
lighter, but the plastic resin is easier for running, so it's a trade-off. The basic rule
of thumb in selecting spikes is to make sure the spikes are more comfortable than
sneakers for running fast on both dirt and grass.

*Source: Narumi Komatsu.

Favorite Gloves and Bats:

Selecting equipment is very personal. I have used the same company—Mizuno—since I played for Orix Blue Wave. Mr. Nobuyoshi Tsubota makes all of my gloves and Mr. Isokazu Kubota (also of Mizuno) makes all of my bats. You'll notice that my gloves are blue and my bats are jet black—a color that is not allowed in Japan but that I switched to when I joined Seattle. I have the designers at Mizuno paint my bats that jet-black color and polish them with two coats to look strong. The bats I use now are made of blue ash, a very strong type of wood that is very durable and does not chip.

Equipment must make you feel confident and self-assured; it is part of the game.

I usually have seven or eight bats at every home game and twice as many on the road—you never know, so be prepared.

One of the things I tell all of my fans is to take good care of their equipment. Show respect to your glove, bats, and spikes—you are counting on them. It has been quite a surprise to see the lack of respect many American baseball players show their equipment

Favorite Shades:

The Oakley model that is now named for me. The "Ichiro" glasses are perfect for baseball, as you can run fast and never worry about them moving out of position, and they look very cool. Equipment—bats, gloves, and spikes—should look cool and get young kids who play baseball to want to wear them.

On How He Became Known Simply as "Ichiro":

Akira Ohgi, my manager with Orix Blue Wave in 1994, suggested that I go by my first name only. At first I thought he was kidding. It took some time to get adjusted to the public address announcer calling me Ichiro instead of Suzuki, but after going on the road I got used to hearing Ichiro.

Batting/Baseball/BP Drills:

The most traditional form of Japanese batting instruction is "toss batting." It involves a hitter and one other person who sits a few feet away and—underhand—tosses balls one after another, which the batter then smashes into a mesh or some sort of netting. The objective of this drill is to get a batter to step and hit with consistency: timing and concentration are the keys to practicing the drill with success.

One of my fondest childhood memories was training to become a better hitter and fielder with the help and guidance of my father. We did this drill throughout my school years. Dad and I trained together; the more I trained, the more I felt the speed of the ball when we played catch was getting too slow. The fungoes he hit me got too easy, so I asked him to hit them harder, and during batting practice I got him to pitch even harder to me.

Favorite Foods:
Onigiri (rice balls), okaka (thin flakes of dried bonito), and pickled plum.

Favorite Hobbies:
Collecting paintings, shopping for antique furniture in San Francisco and Seattle. Driving cars and researching the latest designs in cars (Nissan cars, in particular). Someday perhaps I'll make my own furniture. I'm drawn to anything that's aesthetically pleasing to the eye. But for the most part my favorite thing to do is to stay home with my wife, Yumiko, and our baby.

On His Wedding:
It was at the Riviera Country Club in Los Angeles, a beautiful and private ceremony.

Favorite Pet:
I love my dog—Ikkyu Suzuki.

Favorite Thing About Seattle:
You can see water everywhere you go, which is very unique for an urban area in the States.

Favorite Music:

Hip-hop and rap—my older brother's influence.

Favorite Clothing:

T-shirts, jeans, and suits designed by Yohji Yamamoto.

On Fans in Japan:

I think my fans in Japan are really quality people. When I came to America the number of casual fans went up, but I think the numbers have decreased over the past two years. I get the feeling those [fans] still following me are very determined. My goal is to play up to their expectations. I want all the fans in Japan to stick by me now that I'm in the United States.

One Thing You Don't Like About Japanese Baseball:

Dangerous pitches thrown at the head are problematic.

On Fans in Seattle:

I do appreciate the support they have given me. What I can't express in gratitude with my words, I want to express with my actions on the field—and that's something I will continue to do in the years to come.

HITTING WITH THE OPTIC NERVE

"You can only hit when the information picked up by your optic nerve is processed by your brain and then transmitted accurately to your body. If your eyes can't pick it up, then you can forget about good results."

·

ICHIRO SUZUKI

Ichiro puts his mind into a relaxed and positive mode before the game.

All good hitting begins with finding the release point of a pitcher's delivery—that imaginary box outside of a pitcher's hand. Ted Williams was noted for having such excellent vision that he could see the seams of the baseball spinning on its way to home plate. Jason Giambi of the New York Yankees has made similar claims, and Ichiro Suzuki is no exception to the precept that great hitters are made, not born, through hard work, experimentation, and a fair dose of frustration.

For Ichiro, the process of locating his perfect and seamless hitting groove took a fateful turn when he first visited the Seattle Mariners' spring training camp for two weeks in February and March 1999. One of the players who made the greatest impression on him was Alex Rodriguez, later to be the 2005 MVP with the New York Yankees and one of Ichiro's favorite baseball players.

Introspective and analytical; studying pitchers' release points and arm angles.

"I loved watching Alex and Ken Griffey Jr. play that spring," recalls Ichiro, "and it made my coming to the United States seem more like a real possibility."

Rodriguez remembers standing behind the batting cage and watching in shock as Ichiro hit pitches that most hitters would lunge after and miss.

"Ichiro has a very interesting hitting style: He is aggressive at all times and has an inside-out swing—he would hit the ball sharply to center field by shifting his weight toward his right foot, the one facing the pitcher," said Rodriguez. "Edgar Martinez, a teammate of mine, and later a teammate of Ichiro in Seattle, was also very good at shifting his weight on the swing; since Edgar was batting right-handed, he would move his right leg, the pivot leg, a lot. On curves and sliders he would slide his leg forward to get the timing right. Edgar and Ichiro had a lot in common, though it was a subtle similarity that required careful study.

"But close observation is what allows a hitter to figure out a pitcher. What he

On the path to make a catch at Yankee Stadium.

is throwing, his mannerisms, will tell you things—you want to look him in the eye and try to get a read on where the pitch is going."

After Ichiro returned to Japan, he struggled for several weeks before stumbling upon the ultimate goal of any hitter: gaining the ability to see the ball clearly coming out of the pitcher's hand and to be relaxed and confident enough to make contact based on the information his brain—and optic nerve—were sending to his body. Ichiro remembers telling Alex Rodriguez that "I returned from Arizona to Japan and something was different about my hitting, as I just couldn't seem to be able to follow the ball with my eyes. You don't just hit with your body but with your eyes, and the information that is transmitted is what allows you to hit a fastball coming at 95 mph [or 65 in Little League], or to be able to adjust to a curveball, a slider, a cut fastball.

"You can only hit when the information picked up by your optic nerve is

Ichiro's on-deck circle routine—stretching, thinking, observing.

processed by your brain and then transmitted accurately to your body. If your eyes can't pick it up, then you can forget about good results. And so, on April 11, 1999, I was playing at the Nagoya Dome against the Seibu Lions. I hit a weak grounder off of Yukihiro Nishizaki to second base, and as I was running to first base I suddenly had a strange sensation, a realization I'd found the timing and the swing that I was searching for, not just for months but for several years."

Ichiro has admitted to many Japanese writers, who have been more than a little bit incredulous, that despite seven batting titles with the Orix Blue Wave—.385, .342, .356, .345, .358, .343, and .387—he never had a clear vision of how to

read the release point and coordinate it with his swing until 1999. It was to Ichiro as if those early years of success were a product of hard work and knowledge of pitchers, but never without lingering doubts about his future and the ability to be consistent. The hitting machine was not yet equipped with an owner's manual, so to speak.

Ichiro's swing depends on being able to concentrate all his energy at the point of impact; he has to be able to draw on some method that will allow him to figure out what is off with the swing so he can correct it. After that realization at the Nagoya Dome, Ichiro could finally put all the elements of his swing together,

Loyal fans from Japan come to support Ichiro during his first season with the Mariners.

from start to finish, see the baseball at the release point, and react to it with complete confidence. Narumi Komatsu, a close friend of Ichiro's, relates that Ichiro was like a man given a second chance at life after finding his way through a dark forest.

Says Ichiro: "I was able to come into possession of the special feeling that now allows me to correct any flaws in my batting. I don't believe there could be any greater stroke of luck. It's possible that I could have gone through my entire career fruitlessly searching for it without ever having found it.

"There was a period of trial and error, but never again did I feel like there was no light at the end of the tunnel. Up until then I'd felt as if I'd drifted in and out of grasping that feeling, but now it's as tangible as a mathematical theorem, something I can grasp very clearly. Since I now have the confidence that I'll never be lost again, I won't ever be as anxious as I was in the past.

"To a certain extent baseball's the kind of sport where the stats control you.

Pre-game twilight at Safeco Field in Seattle.

Through 1998, even though I led the league in batting every year, I always felt pressured by stats. But this changed, starting in '99, as I was able to reduce all the stats to just another element in the overall picture and get on with playing the game."

· Chapter ·

ANALYZING ICHIRO'S SWING

"Ichiro is a great pure hitter, a genius at knowing the inner workings of timing, balance, footwork, and strategy. He is a true hitting machine, and I miss the pleasure of seeing him play every day. Most of all I miss the beauty of his swing, because that guy can get to any pitch and then leg it out for a hit."

•

LOU PINIELLA,
FORMER SEATTLE MARINERS MANAGER AND
FOX BASEBALL ANALYST

Ichiro's swing depends on being able to concentrate all his energy at the point of impact.

Baseball "experts" describe Ichiro's swing as unorthodox—so does Ichiro—but a complete step-by-step evaluation reveals that each phase carries with it a purpose that leads to the logical conclusion: Any pitch that seems hittable is worth swinging at.

Step 1 ➤

The swing begins with relaxation and confidence. All hitters use some device to get relaxed in the batter's box. Future Hall of Fame outfielder Tony Gwynn would jerk the bat all over the place to relax.

The legs and feet must be completely relaxed; the hands and wrist are in a relaxed and ready mode. All hitters, from Lou Gehrig to Alex Rodriguez, have devised some method of getting ready to see the pitch and initiate the swing, never raising the elbow.

Ichiro gets set by gripping the bat with his right hand and winding his arm around in a sweeping motion, as if to take in everyone watching him on the diamond. He then pauses—barely—with the bat out in front, pointing in the direction of the pitcher. This is a relaxation method of setting himself at the plate and getting ready to watch the pitcher to see what he's going to throw.

Ichiro gets set by gripping the bat with his
right hand and winding his arm around
in a sweeping motion.

Ichiro takes a parallel stance—the front foot is in
front of the plate and the back foot is behind the plate.

Step 2 ➤

Ichiro takes a parallel stance: The front foot is in front of the plate and the back foot is behind the plate. Other possible stances: Standing near the front of the batter's box helps when trying to bunt for a base hit or when trying to catch a pitch before it breaks — one possible way of dealing with a knuckleball pitcher like Steve Sparks. Standing near the back of the batter's box will give a hitter a longer look at the pitch — and he won't have to commit to the pitch as quickly.

Two other common stances are the open and the closed stance. In the open stance, the back foot is closer to the plate than is the front foot; it is often used by hitters struggling to see pitches on the inner half of the plate. In the closed stance, the front foot is closer to the plate than the back foot, which makes it easier to hit outside pitches but tougher to hit inside pitches.

Ichiro preaches that it's best to be ready to adjust — moving back if necessary to hit a curveball or getting lower in the stance to get a piece of the ball on tough pitches, especially on down and away strikes from sinkerball pitchers.

Step 3 ➤

Ichiro takes a comfortable grip on the bat: The middle knuckles of the fingers will be in perfect alignment. Some hitters will choke up on the bat to slap pitches down the line or to improve the ability to drop a bunt down.

Step 4 ➤

Ichiro looks for the release point: The right foot stays on the ground and the left leg (the pivot leg) acts as the trigger to getting set to generate the movement of the bat. Ichiro used to lift his right leg in Japan, but that timing device was eliminated because American pitchers are much quicker to deliver the baseball. Japanese hurlers tend to be more deliberate, walking around the mound, grabbing rosin bags, simply taking an extra beat or two before breaking the hands from the glove and delivering the pitch.

He takes a comfortable grip on the bat before looking for the release
point. The right foot stays on the ground and the left foot acts as
a trigger to generate the movement of the bat.

Ichiro believes that this change did not impact his hitting form in any significant way, despite what many Japanese journalists believed after noticing it in 2001: "The process of getting set [at the plate] isn't accomplished by raising the right leg, but [by] what the batter does with the left leg. It [getting set to hit] takes place in your adductor muscles and the muscles on the inside of the knee."

Step 5

Ichiro initiates the movement of the swing as his hips and hands come together to drive through to the point of contact with the baseball.

Ichiro initiates the movement of the swing as his hips
and hands come togeter to drive through to the
point of contact with the baseball.

At the end of the swing—after the point of contact, he completes his
follow-through and the hands finish high.

Step 6

As hips and hands come together, the weight shifts from the pivot (back) leg,
through the middle to the point of contact.

Step 7 ➤

At the end of the swing—after the point of contact—Ichiro completes his follow-through and the hands finish high. Despite all the comments from so-called baseball experts that the swing is hard to emulate, this swing is not the least bit out of character with the standard mechanics taught by most hitting instructors in major league-baseball.

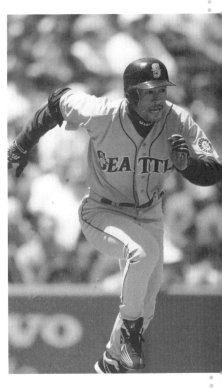

Ichiro breaks into his running form and begins the race to first base—he can do this in 3.6 seconds!

THE ESSENTIAL ELEMENTS OF HITTING

"When you're trying to pick up the path of the ball coming toward you, pick it up first as a line, then as a point."

•

KENICHIRO KAWAMURA,
COACH OF ICHIRO'S MINOR-LEAGUE TEAM

The seamless and pure ease with which Ichiro swings the bat belies the hard work and dedication he's followed as his mantra to ensure his pro-baseball success in Japan and in the United States.

His father, Nobuyuki Suzuki, was a talented amateur baseball player and totally devoted to his son. Father and son were regulars at the neighborhood Airport Batting Center, a mecca where top prep stars could strut their stuff in front of their peers.

Ichiro eschewed bravado in favor of humbly putting into practice the work ethic he was learning from his father and his high school coach, Go Nakamura, who openly wondered, "How can someone so scrawny play baseball?"

Ichiro's response was to exercise (he stayed right around 150–160 pounds) and drink milk. (He grew several inches to reach his current height of five feet nine inches).

When the time came to determine whether he'd pitch—"In junior high I think I had a decent fastball"—or play a position on a full-time basis, something completely out of his control took a hand in deciding his baseball future. While riding around the campus of Meiden High School, one of the top prep baseball programs in Japan, a car cruised into him in a violent collision and knocked him off his bike. The injuries destroyed his pitching form; Ichiro had to learn how to throw all over again, and while he could still fire strikes from right field to third base, he was somehow never able to recapture the mechanics of his pitching delivery that had allowed him to throw a good sinking fastball as a junior high school student.

Ichiro's high school experience was not without the usual high jinks that go on at any prep school—whether in Japan, England, or Deerfield, Massachusetts. As Ichiro recalls, "It was scary when the upperclassmen got mad at you because they'd make you sit on garbage cans *seiza* style [on your knees with all the weight of your body bearing down on the lower part of your legs]."

And to think this punishment was for a simple faux pas such as being caught eating soft-serve ice cream cones or not rinsing the rice properly in the dining halls.

Ichiro was tabbed a fourth-round draft pick in 1999, by the Orix Blue Wave, of the Pacific Coast League. The Kobe, Japan, organization selected him based on the scouting reports of the late Katsutoshi Miwata. In fact, Miwata was one of the few people in the organization who was at the same time both honest and supportive. Miwata, for instance, impressed Ichiro with the need for physical conditioning and the strengthening of his abdominals. To this day Ichiro follows a daily regimen of sit-ups and other calisthenics and stretching exercises.

Once thrust into professional baseball as his career of choice, Ichiro was able to articulate and master several instructional techniques that have made him arguably the best hitter in the world today.

1. IMITATE THE HITTING STYLE OF PLAYERS YOU LIKE TO WATCH ON TV

Ichiro imitated the inside-out swing of southpaw batter Kazunori Shinozuka of the Tokyo Giants, and it paid huge dividends.

Keith Hernandez, a great left-handed hitter of the '80s and '90s with the St. Louis Cardinals and New York Mets, imitated the swing of Willie McCovey of the San Francisco Giants. "He was the one hitter who always made an impact on me, who gave me a visual model to follow in perfecting my own unique swing. But I needed that visual role model, and it helped me make steady, incremental progress early on in my career."

Ichiro has always followed this same path to success: "Imitating the inside-out swing of Shinozuka [a hitter who hit sharp liners to center or left instead of pulling the ball to right] made me what I am today. I was not consciously aware that by imitating Shinozuka I was practicing the inside-out swing [the swing that features "going the other way" or simply hitting the ball to all fields], and it worked out well for me.

"If you are in a slump, and this is especially true for children who are not locked into a particular hitting form or style of hitting, then imitating other hitters may give you just the spark you need to improve."

2. LEARN FROM YOUR MISTAKES AT THE PLATE

John Olerud, one of the best left-handed hitters in the game, says Ichiro passed many tidbits of wisdom along to him, and many of the other hitters, in the Seattle clubhouse:

"Always concentrate on each pitch you face over the course of the game with complete intensity, focus, and concentration. But never allow adversity to have an effect on your mood and disposition from one at-bat to the next."

3. HIT TO ALL FIELDS AND LEARN HOW TO HIT THE CURVEBALL BY "BUILDING THE WALL"

The Japanese have a phrase, *nimai goshi*, which can be translated into English as "doubling the strength of the lower half of the body." Ichiro explained in an interview last season how this translates into his style of hitting with his unique inside-out swing: "Many young left-handed hitters, especially when facing a left-handed pitcher, will see a big breaking ball as if it were coming from behind—as if it might hit you square in the back—and the tendency is to hesitate for a split second. By pulling back for an instant, you will miss the chance to hit that pitch.

"And so I created the mental image of a wall on my right side [since Ichiro is a left-handed hitter]. Once the mental image of the wall is in place, I can hit to all fields—right, center, and left—and this process of building the wall takes time to practice. That's the main reason why I'd hit the ball to left field early in the spring, as the natural tendency is to be more conscious of the zone to the left of center—and that's why I often hit the ball that way in April."

Ichiro unveiled this technique in the spring of 2001, his first camp with the Mariners, and Lou Piniella and his coach, Sam Perlozzo (now the manager of the Baltimore Orioles), could not figure out why an accomplished hitter (the winner of seven batting titles) was hitting everything to left.

"It reached the point where we had to start wondering whether Ichiro would ever hit a pitch to center, which was what he was famous for in Japan," said Perlozzo. "But one day the hits to center and right started coming, and that's when we knew that he had really arrived."

Pineilla has his own view of "building the wall." "I was just waiting to see him hit pitches to right that were meant to be pulled—I don't want him pulling pitches that are meant to be hit up the middle, but once the balls started coming off his bat to right, I knew I had nothing more that needed to be said to Ichiro."

SITUATIONAL HITTING 101

Ichiro, like all good hitters at all levels of competition, has acquired the skill to hit the ball where it is pitched: outside pitches to left, inside to right. That is, once he has "built the wall" to allow him to hit to all fields.

Keith Hernandez, National League MVP in 1982 with the St. Louis Cardinals, cautions against hitting coaches who will try to get a player to hit every pitch to the opposite field. In his excellent book *If at First . . . ,* Hernandez brings up this exchange with the Cards' special batting instructor Harry "the Hat" Walker: "After a good spring [in 1975] I got off to a terrible start, hitting .230 after two weeks of the season . . . Walker was working with the Card hitters, and for two weeks he coached me every day on hitting to the opposite field. That's how he hit; that's how he thought everyone should. But I had grown up hitting the ball where it was pitched: outside to left, inside to right. Dad threw thousands of pitches to me and made certain I hit to all fields. Now I was being told to hit everything to left. Walker's coaching, well meaning as it was, set me back. It amazes me to realize how difficult it was to break the habits created by Harry the Hat. It was three or four years before I was really comfortable pulling the ball again."

Ichiro's dad also threw him countless pitches to enable him to hit to all fields. The payback in the real world was to be able to hit behind a runner trying to steal; to pull the ball to second to move a runner over; to drive a tough pitch that most hitters can't reach to center on a line; to go the other way—to left field for a lefty swinger—on a tough outside pitch. But back in 2001 Ichiro had to "build the wall" before he could showcase the form that won him seven batting crowns.

Ichiro was mildly bemused about this concern of the Mariners' coaching staff. But he offers some useful advice for young players on how to deal with these sorts of "concerns" from managers, teammates, parents, and friends.

"You need to go about your business, coping with the issues you need to address as a baseball player, but ultimately it is your responsibility to instill in your manager and your teammates the confidence that you can handle your assignment. The ideal is to demonstrate through what you achieve on the field that you can handle it, even if you don't discuss it with them very much."

THE DELICATE ART OF BUNTING

Ichiro is one of the best bunters in the world today, preferring to use the drag bunt as his main weapon against the pitcher and unwary infielders. Bunting has become a lost art in baseball. Ichiro is one of the few players in the game who understands how to do it right—to be soft with the bat, as if you are catching the ball, to let the pitch come to you—and how effective it can be at disrupting the defense and throwing the pitcher out of whack.

STANCE 1. The Sacrifice Bunt: Square away to bunt by pivoting on the back foot. A left-handed hitter places his hand just below the trademark on the bat with the right hand on the handle. For a righty hitter, it's just the opposite. Move the top hand up the trademark; think of the top hand as a fulcrum, while the bottom hand directs the movement of the bat as it makes contact with the ball.

STANCE 2. The Ichiro Drag Bunt: Same getting-set device as for a regular swing: The bat is pointed directly in front of the batter's box, facing the pitcher. In a drag bunt you are literally taking the ball with you as you run down the baseline; however, the ball is not tracking straight down the line with you. A right-handed hitter has two options: either bunting the ball toward third base or placing the ball toward first base.

There's a common misconception that a drag bunt is supposed to be pushed (or dragged) down the line; the actual goal is to bunt the ball between the pitcher and first baseman, creating confusion over who will cover the bag.

The form: Ichiro goes from his setup position. He has his right hand

on the handle and the left hand firmly on the trademark. He pivots on his back foot and places the ball between the pitcher and first baseman.

TWO OTHER COMMON BUNTING VARIATIONS

3. **The Slug Bunt:** Square away to bunt, but with your hands below the trademark on the bat. Pull the bat back (or bring the bottom hand up) to chop the ball on the ground for an infield hit.

4. **The Swinging Bunt:** Offer to bunt but pull the bat back and take a full swing. Many times the third baseman will break toward home plate, anticipating the bunt, and you can hit the ball into left field for a single or a double down the line.

THE TWO "CONTRADICTORY" ELEMENTS OF HITTING

Alex Rodriguez has said that Ichiro's ability to hit over .300 with more than 200 hits every year (and he may yet make it to .400) is a combination of technical skill, knowledge of pitchers and their quirks, and his ability to hit pitches that most batters would either spit on or miss by a mile.

"Ichiro is one of the most aggressive hitters in baseball," said Rodriguez, "and yet he is able to drive any pitch—whether inside, outside, curveball, fastball, or slider. He somehow balances patience with his aggressive swing."

Ichiro sorts out this seeming contradiction. Keep in mind that he faces more regular-season pitches on average in any given year than any other hitter in Japan or America because he rarely walks and bats leadoff.

"Well, there are two important elements in batting. There's a part that needs to be aggressive and a part that needs to be patient. These are contradictory elements, but unless you can be both, there will be an imbalance in your batting. If one element is stronger than the other, say the aggressive part, then you'll chase pitches you don't really want to go after. If the patient part is stronger, you won't go after pitches you could hit. But as long as both of these fundamentals are working together, your hitting will be in perfect balance and you will always be able to do well against all types of pitches and pitchers.

"For most of my career I have kept these two elements in balance, but in the

second half of 2002 and during 2003 I started to struggle as I came closer to the 200-hit mark. As I got closer to the goal, I lost control of my batting and lost my focus. This experience showed me that keeping the delicate balance between the two elements of hitting is something I have to always pay close attention to, as the goal is to stay consistent."

Alex Rodriguez: "Ichiro is one of the most aggressive hitters in baseball, and yet he is able to drive any pitch—whether inside, outside, curveball, fastball, or slider. He somehow balances patience with an aggressive swing."

Ichiro gets set in the batter's box . . .

before pivoting on his back foot . . .

and shifting his weight through the middle to the point
of contact, before completing his follow-through . . .

as the hands finish high.

Despite comments from so-called baseball experts that this
swing is hard to emulate, Ichiro's swing is not the least bit out
of character with the standard mechanics taught by most
hitting instructors in major-league baseball.

FLAWLESS FIELDING MADE SIMPLE

"I think one way I surprised the fans in America is with my defense and throwing. I always look forward to the way the fans in the right field stands react. I like how excited they get. The last few years in Japan I didn't get that same reaction from the crowd because they'd taken a kind of 'been there, seen that' reaction to my defensive play."

•

ICHIRO SUZUKI

Ichiro lost his ability to throw a baseball for a brief period after his auto accident in high school. Unfazed by this setback—though it determined he'd place more of his attention on hitting rather than pitching—he had to methodically rebuild his arm strength through constant throwing practice, endless repetition. He started doing long-toss drills every day, working on the mechanics of the throwing motion, and in a matter of months he could duplicate the laser-beam throws that are now his bread and butter as a five-time Gold Glove outfielder.

Proper throwing mechanics require a simple, natural motion: When the throwing side goes back to generate the force of releasing the baseball, the other side of the body naturally pops up. As you initiate the throw, regardless of whether it's from an infield or an outfield position, pull your nonthrowing side down. The throwing side of the body will come right over the top.

ICHIRO'S THROWING MOTION FROM START TO FINISH

1. The front (left) side of the body goes up; the right (back) leg is used as pivoting device (remember that Ichiro throws right-handed).
2. The throwing arm goes into the slot—the elbow is bent.
3. The arm starts to come over the top—the forearm is perpendicular to the upper arm; then he pulls the front side (glove hand) down and the right arm follows through (from knee height to past the body) on the deceleration phase of the throw.

Of course, a correct across-the-seams grip on the baseball will still determine the accuracy of the throw, as it is the only grip to allow for precise location. Ichiro's perfect throwing form includes several checkpoints: He never opens up his front side because this would reduce the velocity of the throw, a big problem on a long throw from right or center to third or home. "Opening up" means that your front shoulder stays down—rather than coming back up, as you pull the throwing side back.

Here are two drills to understand the shoulder position on the throw. There are two things to remember in these drills. (1) Practice the throwing motion in front of a mirror so that you can actually see what your arm looks like during the throwing motion. You could also have a coach or friend videotape or take digital photos of your shoulder motion so that you can fine-tune your mechanical flaws. (2) Next time you watch Ichiro play, whether on TV or at the game, stay focused on analyzing how he completes the throw—both to the cutoff man and to the different bags.

Remember that it is impossible to generate arm speed from the "open" position. That's the main reason why young outfielders can't seem to put any juice on their throws.

Ichiro's throwing motion:
As you initiate the throw,
regardless of whether
it's from an infield or an
outfield position, pull the
nonthrowing side down
and the throwing side
of the body will come
right over the top.

The Long-Toss Drill

This drill, favored by Ichiro and most major leaguers, improves both mechanics and arm strength. Throw the ball back and forth, starting out about 10 to 15 yards apart, with one of the other players on your team. Gradually increase the distance to stretch out the muscles; move as far back as your arm strength will allow (until you start one-hopping your throws). Focus on proper mechanics with every throw. Don't get into bad habits by not rehearsing the ideal throwing motion and placing the proper grip on the baseball.

Ichiro practices the long-toss drill with the other Mariners outfielders between innings, before the game, and of course in spring training to build arm strength for the long season.

The Throwing-the-Baseball-Across-the-Seams Drill

A typical mistake of a young outfielder is to casually grip the ball with the fingers along the seams. One way to prevent this mistake is to grab as many balls you can get your hands on and make throws—10 to 15 to second base, 10 to 15 to third base, and 10 to 15 to home plate—to a teammate with the correct grip. Focus on how you are gripping the baseball.

FIELDING THE BASEBALL

Ichiro advises to put your body in front of the ball so it won't get past you and roll to the wall, and to field it cleanly before starting to initiate the throw with the upper body. Don't charge too aggressively on a one-hopper or you may never be able to field it cleanly. One option is to drop down on one knee to field the ball, but that (as Ichiro would argue) is a personal matter.

Ichiro making another classic catch—put your body in front of the ball so it won't get past you and roll to the wall and field it cleanly before starting to initiate the throw with the upper body.

On the run after reading the ball off of the bat.

READING THE BALL OFF THE BAT

Ichiro preaches that you need to try to figure out a hitter's tendency to hit the ball to different fields, and whether he tends to drive the ball to the gap. He used to talk about fielding with former teammate Mike Cameron, a brilliant fielder in his own right. "The plan for an outfielder is to get as much detailed information as possible on how a hitter will hit on certain types of pitches. When major leaguers hit the baseball—and this is often true in high school if the hitters are pretty good—there's a spin on the ball as it comes off the bat. It can be very diffi-

Wearing the classic Ichiro Oakley shades; always
keeping his eye on the ball to make the clean catch.

cult to analyze all this visual information, and that makes it a challenge to field
the baseball. But after a while you can really see the impact different styles of
hitting have on how the ball comes off the bat. There are a lot of players who
drive the ball [such as Gary Sheffield of the Yankees who has tremendous bat
speed] and other players who hit it in a way that makes it go farther than you'd
anticipate. It's up to you to be able pay attention to the little details when you are
standing in the outfield."

ON MAKING SURE YOU KNOW WHAT'S GOING ON IN THE GAME——AND WHAT'S GOING ON IN YOUR LIFE

In an interview with his friend Narumi Komatsu, Ichiro credits his high school coach, Go Nakamura on understanding the importance of all the little things that make a great baseball player—hitting in the clutch, being a selfless teammate, always keeping your head in the game, and making the right decisions—where to throw the baseball, when to steal a base to help the team win: "He's the greatest teacher I've ever had. He taught me baseball, of course, but so much more. He taught me how to act when I went out into the world. He taught me a lot of life lessons during our team meetings, saying that you'll only be able to play baseball for a short time, but the real issue is what kind of person you'll be after that. What I remember most are two things he said, 'Aim at being a regular in life more than a regular at baseball,' and 'Strive to surpass your master.'"

ICHIRO'S RELATIONSHIP WITH HIS COACHES

The Seattle Mariners' coaches learned the first season that Ichiro is quite brilliant when it comes to knowing how to react to a ball on the fly in a specific game situation. "He's as intelligent as any player I've ever met in the game of baseball," said Perlozzo.

Three different approaches to tracking down the ball, but the fundamentals of fielding apply—it is up to you to be able to pay attention to the little details when you are standing in the outfield.

Chapter

STEALING WINS
WITH STEALS

"With base stealing, how many bases you steal doesn't matter. What matters is in what kind of situation you steal. There are times when stealing a base might help you win the game, and times when it doesn't affect the outcome of the game and only adds to your personal base-stealing stats."

•

ICHIRO SUZUKI

A quick check of Ichiro's base-stealing stats bears out the point that stealing is a matter of picking spots that will help the team win games. Meaningless steals to pad stats is a selfish way to play the game and the complete opposite of Ichiro's team-comes-first philosophy.

Ichiro's stolen-base numbers vary from year to year (with a low of 11 with the Orix Blue Wave in 1998 and a career high of 56 with the Seattle Mariners in 2001, depending on how many chances he gets to steal in situations that contribute wins to his team.

Base stealing that helps produce meaningful runs is what Ichiro calls "quality" base stealing. There's no point in building stats that don't translate into wins. The Ichiro mantra on when to steal goes something like this: "If you're going after the base-stealing crown, then everyone expects you to steal. But if you suddenly start running on your own for no apparent reason, then people will wonder what the heck is going on with you."

Ichiro taking a lead, eye on the pitcher.   Ichiro breaking for second, watching the ball.

THE ART OF THE STEAL

The first thing to do is to check with your manager to see how stealing fits in with the overall strategy of the game. Lou Piniella would almost always hand Ichiro the green light (the freedom to run on his own) in Seattle back in 2001 (when he stole 56 bases), but Ichiro still advises a team-oriented approach to making the ultimate decision:

- **When to go:** If the manager tells you to steal in any situation, you can go for it with abandon. But if you are told to steal only when there's a 100 percent chance you'll be safe, it would be better to avoid taking any risks.

- **How to steal:** Your only worry is how the pitcher is holding you on base. Keep in mind that pitchers practice all the time to prevent steals from the set—no wind-up—position.

Ichiro running while looking toward home plate.

- **How to read the pitcher:** See if you can find a pattern that will tip off when a pitcher will throw over to first base or whether a pitcher will throw home, allowing you to get a good jump. Watch the pitcher's glove, his head, his hands, his body language—anything to give you more information about what he might do. The goal is to find a rhythm, a pattern, in the pitcher's delivery. That will give you a distinct advantage.

- **Be aggressive on the bases:** You can't be afraid to get thrown out. Ichiro swiped 56 bags in 2001—his first season with Seattle—because he was unfazed by a "caught stealing" on his stat sheet. He could steal successfully on both Barry Zito—blessed with a very good pick-off move—and Orlando "El Duque" Hernandez, though he takes forever to get through his leg kick to deliver the pitch, because Ichiro knows how to follow the advice of all the great base stealers: "Don't let the fear of failure limit your chance of success."

- **Take a lead that allows you to get a good jump:** Don't stray too far or you could get picked off of first base. Experiment with a four-step lead to see if this distance will give you enough ground to both steal the base and to get back to the bag if the pitcher throws to first. You can also take a five-or-six-step lead if you are pretty sure the pitcher isn't paying attention to you. This happens more often than you'd expect, even if perceived as a genuine base-stealing threat.

- **Never cross your legs over each other as the pitcher throws over to first** or you will never get back to the bag. Never turn your back to the bag as you take your lead or you are a sitting duck on any decent pick-off throw.

- **Use your speed and run with perfect form:** Use your arms to assist the legs to generate acceleration, and slide into

second base. Says Ichiro: "When the catcher makes his usual throw to second and the runner's safe, it always means the runner has picked up the pitcher's delivery. Don't forget to look over at the catcher for clues about pitch outs—the pitcher and catcher are working together to prevent you from stealing the base. And when you run look briefly toward home plate so you know where the ball is."

ICHIRO ON HEADS-UP BASERUNNING

Here's a transcription of a conversation Ichiro shared after checking with Piniella about how to handle certain baserunning scenarios: When in doubt, figure out what's really going on around you on the field.

"You'll often have a situation where you have to make a choice on how to handle a certain play. It's important for a player to know how his manager or coach expects him to react. Let's say a fly ball is hit to the deepest part of the stadium. I'm on second base, with no outs. I'm not sure if the ball will be caught or will get past the outfielder for a double at least. What should I do?

"There are two ways to play this: I could wait near the bag so I can tag up easily. I could go halfway down the baseline so that if it gets through I can score. It's up to the runner to figure out how to handle these choices. If you're thrown out, it will be your own fault, and everyone on the team will wonder what the heck you were doing.

"In the case where there're no outs and I'm on second base and stay fairly close to the bag, if the next hitter gets a double, the best I can do is to advance to third. If I proceed halfway down the basepath I can score. Choices. There are two ways to play this, and I would let my manager know I want a clear sign—so I don't make a mistake that might cost us the game."

IDEAL RUNNING FORM AROUND THE BASES

Can any player beat Ichiro's time of 3.6 seconds from home to first? Has anyone in the history of the game been able to use his speed as a weapon more effec-
tively than Ichiro?

No, and no. And at times he does endeavor to beat out infield hits just because
of his electric speed and the disruptive impact it has on the flow of the game.
"Pitchers in America throw a lot of breaking balls that are similar to the fork-

Ichiro's perfect running form—relying on the arms to
help the legs generate maximum speed.

balls in Japan. These pitches sink, and so the tendency is to hit the ball on the
ground. There's also a wider strike zone on the outside part of the plate in the
United States, and that means a lot of infield grounders, and I'll do my best to
beat the throw."

Running from the Batter's Box to First Base

- Your arms are in an L-shape and held in close to the sides. The upper half of your body is leaning forward.

- Use your arms to help push your body along the baseline. Think of putting one foot in front of the other. Run with a fluid motion like a jaguar or a puma.

- Take a straight line to first base on an infield grounder. Hit the inside corner of the bag with good body lean. If you hit a single to center, take a small loop about five feet from the first-base bag and get ready to head to second base.

- As you round second—if the ball is hit to the outfield, a liner to right-center, for instance—be aggressive and think about turning the single into a double. You will probably know when you're a step or two past first whether or not you can make it to the second-base bag without being thrown out. If the outfielder has a strong arm and fields the ball without any problems, there's still plenty of time to head back to first base and start thinking about stealing second.

Always out of the batter's box in a flash—the best contact hitter in baseball today steals hits from fielders who are not prepared for his quickness and acceleration.

As you round any base, be aggressive and think about turning a single into a double and a double into a triple.

Tagging Up Without Fear

"On tag plays at the plate you don't want to go flying in the air because the catcher blocked you out and you're tossed about. If you get blocked like that, you get worn out. You usually can see it happening in advance—that you'll be sent flying—and the best way to avoid that is to time your start from the bag in such a way as to avoid the collision and slide around—not into—the tag."

Sliding into Second After the Steal

Step 1

You need a quality feetfirst slide to complete the steal. Take the lead. Sprint 10 to 11 steps in a low-center-of-gravity posture toward second base. When you are about three steps from the bag, break down into your slide (rather than flying), and head straight to the bag. Tuck one leg under and just point the other leg toward the bag.

When you are about three steps from the bag, break down into your
slide and head straight to the bag. Tuck one leg under and just
point the other leg toward the bag. As you get to second,
lean your body forward and use your bent leg.

Step 2

As you get to second base, lean your body forward and use your bent leg to push up. Of course, you are often sliding into the bag with the second baseman or the shortstop in your way, so keep your eyes open. Be careful not to get hurt and collide with the fielder.

Step 3

The pop-up slide, favored by Freddie Patek and Willie Wilson of the Kansas City Royals in the '70s and '80s, Tony Gwynn in the '90s, and Ichiro, of course, in 2006, allows the hands to help your legs get through the slide, and then you can simply pop up—should the ball get past the shortstop who is covering—and sprint to the next base. This is also the best slide on plays at the plate, a much safer option than the headfirst variety that Rickey Henderson made his calling card.

Running to second on another
successful steal attempt.

Chapter

THE CULT
OF ICHIRO

The vast majority of major-league baseball players treat Ichiro as a breed apart, a rare once-in-a-generation talent. He may not have the physical stature of a George Brett or a Stan Musial, but he is as good a hitter, and as true a person, as the game has ever seen.

On the night that he broke the single-season hit record of George Sisler in 2004—a record that had stood supreme for ninety years—his fellow countryman Hideki Matsui of the New York Yankees put everything into perspective about how special Ichiro is to baseball and its lore: "He is the best hitter I have ever watched, either in Japan or the United States," said Matsui. "His ability to put the barrel of the bat on the ball is uncanny. He is an unbelievable talent, and baseball as a sport is blessed to have such a tremendous person to build around for the future."

A ROUNDUP OF TRADITIONAL BASEBALL DRILLS

BATTING

The Batting Tee

The primary goal of this drill is to develop consistent form and to learn to spray the ball to all fields.

1. Stand close to the tee if you want to hit the ball the other way. You will be at or behind the plate as you make contact.

2. Don't stand directly on top of the tee if you want to learn how to pull the ball; instead, move the tee so that when you swing you will be able to get the head of your bat out to where the ball is resting on the tee.

3. Move the tee around to the various positions to duplicate different pitch

locations in a game. The angle of the bat will determine where you will hit the ball.

4. Hitting to left field: make contact with the ball as you face the tee.
5. Hitting to center field: make contact with the tee moved slightly forward.
6. Hitting to right field: make contact with the tee moved well forward.
7. Practice hitting the top half of the ball to hit line drives and grounders. If you make contact with the bottom half of the ball, the result is high pop flies and easy outs.

REPETITIONS: *Shoot for 100 swings per workout.*

Soft Toss

A very popular drill in both Japan and the Americas. One player sits with a bucket of baseballs and tosses each ball underhanded to the hitter working on his swing. Try to set up some netting to catch the baseballs. Toss the balls to every part of the hitting zone—down and in, down and away, inside and up, inside and low—to force a hitter to make all the essential adjustments.

1. Practice hitting the top half of the baseball.
2. Regardless of whether you're hitting to left, center, or right, the ball should still end up in the net.

REPETITIONS: *Shoot for 100 swings per workout.*

One-Knee Drill

Drop down on one knee and work on your top hand only. This drill forces you to hit the top half of the baseball. The one limitation is that it only addresses the upper half of your body.

REPETITIONS: *Shoot for 25 swings per workout.*

Hitting Machines

Take 100 swings against a pitching machine at the local batting range, always increasing velocity after 25 pitches.

Batting Practice

A live pitcher is always preferable to a pitching machine. You need to see the release point from a "live" pitcher. But at any level, the batting practice pitcher will throw well below the velocity and the quality of any pitcher you will face in a game. Use your swings in BP to work your way around the diamond:

- Hit 10 balls to left field.
- Hit 10 balls to center field.
- Hit 10 balls to right field.

REPETITIONS: *Repeat if time allows.*

Practice Swings

This is what you do in the on-deck circle during the game. Work with your hitting coach on the side to practice your swing, with or without doughnuts (weights) to make the swing feel lighter and to gain more confidence as you head to the plate.

REPETITIONS: *Take 10 to 20 practice swings per day.*

RUNNING DRILLS FOR SPEED

Forget distance running; baseball is a sport of short bursts of acceleration. Do 10 x 80 yard sprints; 8 x 60 yard sprints; and 6 x 40 yard sprints. Do this on a track or on the practice field. Have a coach or friend time each sprint, and always try to eclipse your personal best. Remember to maintain perfect running form on each sprint.

THROWING DRILLS FOR ENDURANCE

Long-Toss Drill

Start by throwing the ball back and forth with a friend—about 12 to 15 yards apart. Gradually increase the distance to stretch out your arm. Continue to move farther apart until you start bouncing your throws.

Base Drills

Grab a bucket filled with 75 balls and throw (with an across-the-seams grip) 25 balls to a teammate standing at second base, 25 balls to a teammate standing at third base, and 25 balls to home plate. Rehearse this drill while running full speed to make the throw.

REPETITIONS: *Repeat 2 to 3 times per week.*

Fungo Drills

Jimmie Reese, a former coach with the California Angels, is the best fungo hitter in the history of baseball. Reese would do the following drill to improve the instincts of his fielders.

Hit 10 balls to right; 10 balls to center; 10 balls to left—each fungo will force the fielder to extend himself a little more to make a catch—whether to break in on a shallow blooper or break back on a liner to the fence.

Dave Garcia, who managed the Cleveland Indians in the '70s, was also an excellent fungo hitter. "During spring training I keep extending the fielders gradually so that they begin to realize how far they can really go," said Garcia. "But before a game I never try to cross up an infielder. I try to make him look good by giving him a ball he can handle."

Fungo form: Reese explained in an interview from the '70s how to hit a fungo:

"If I want to hit grounders, I hit the ball while it's between my waist and knees. If I want to pop one straight up for a catcher to work on foul flies—and that's the toughest fungo to hit—I have to throw the ball over my head and come under it. And if I'm hitting flies to the outfielders, the ball is only slightly above my head so I can get distance. If you want line drives, it's out to the side so that you can strike it good."

Ichiro in the batter's box.

APPENDIX 2

THE ICHIRO SUZUKI FILE

Number 51

OUTFIELDER: *Seattle Mariners*

DATE OF BIRTH: *October 22, 1973*

AGE: *32*

BIRTHPLACE: *Kasugai, Aichi, Japan*

HEIGHT: *5'9"*

WEIGHT: *160 pounds*

BATS: *Left*

THROWS: *Right*

THE JAPAN STAT LINE

YEAR	TEAM	AVG	HR	RBI	AB	H	BB	SB
1992	Orix Blue Wave	.253	0	5	95	24	9	3
1993	Orix Blue Wave	.188	1	3	64	12	4	0
1994	Orix Blue Wave	.385	13	54	546	210	111	29
1995	Orix Blue Wave	.342	25	80	524	179	104	49
1996	Orix Blue Wave	.356	16	84	542	193	104	35
1997	Orix Blue Wave	.345	17	91	536	185	94	39
1998	Orix Blue Wave	.358	13	71	506	181	79	11
1999	Orix Blue Wave	.343	21	68	411	141	80	12
2000	Orix Blue Wave	.387	12	73	395	153	73	21

THE SEATTLE MARINERS STAT LINE

YEAR	AGE	G	AB	R	H	2B	3B	HR	RBI	SB	CS	BB	SO	BA	OBP	SLG
2001	27	157	692	127	242	34	8	8	69	56	14	30	53	.350	.381	.457
2002	28	157	647	111	208	27	8	8	51	31	15	68	62	.321	.388	.425
2003	29	159	679	111	212	29	8	13	62	34	8	36	69	.312	.352	.436
2004	30	161	704	101	262	24	5	8	60	36	11	49	63	.372	.414	.455
2005	31	162	679	111	206	21	12	15	68	33	8	48	66	.303	.350	.436

5 Seasons

		796	3401	561	1130	135	41	52	310	190	56	231	313	.332	.377	.442

RATING ICHIRO BY THE NUMBERS

**ALL-STAR GAMES: FIVE APPEARANCES,
2001–2005**

Awards

2001—AMERICAN LEAGUE MVP
2001—AMERICAN LEAGUE ROOKIE OF THE YEAR

GOLD GLOVES (5): 2001–2005

SILVER SLUGGER: 2001

Ichiro's Top Ten Rankings in the American League

Numbers in parentheses indicate rank.

BATTING AVERAGE
2001 .350 (1)
2002 .321 (4)
2003 .312 (7)
2004 .372 (1)

**CAREER BATTING AVERAGE = .332
(THIRD AMONG ACTIVE PLAYERS)**

ON-BASE PERCENTAGE
2002 .388 (10)
2004 .414 (2)

GAMES
2002 157 (9)
2004 161 (3)
2005 162 (1)

AT-BATS
2001 692 (1)
2002 647 (3)
2003 679 (2)
2004 704 (1)
2005 679 (1)

RUNS
2001 127 (2)
2002 111 (9)
2003 111 (7)
2005 111 (9)

HITS[a]
2001 242 (1)[b]
2002 208 (2)
2003 212 (2)

2004 262 (1)[c]
2005 206 (2)

TOTAL BASES
2001 316 (9)
2004 320 (6)

TRIPLES
2001 8 (7)
2002 8 (3)
2003 8 (8)
2005 12 (2)

STOLEN BASES
2001 56 (1)
2002 31 (4)
2003 34 (5)
2004 36 (2)
2005 33 (5)

SINGLES
2001 192 (1)
2002 165 (1)
2003 162 (1)
2004 225 (1)
2005 158 (1)

[a] In 2001, Ichiro collected a hit in 135 games, matching a big-league record held by Rogers "Rajah" Hornsby (1922), Chuck Klein (1930), Wade Boggs (1985), and Derek Jeter (1999).

[b] On September 29, 2001, Ichiro broke the ninety-year-old MLB rookie hit mark of 233 held by Shoeless Joe Jackson.

[c] All-time single-season hit record.

TIMES ON BASE

2001 280 (4)

2002 281 (4)

2003 254 (10)

2004 315 (1)

2005 258 (6)

INTENTIONAL WALKS

2001 10 (8)

2002 27 (1)

2004 19 (1)

2005 23 (2)

AT-BATS PER STRIKEOUT

2001 13.1 (1)

2002 10.4 (4)

2003 9.8 (7)

2004 11.2 (3)

2005 10.3 (5)

INDEX